LOVE OF DOGS

DR. MICHAEL MILLER

Copyright ©2024 Dr. Michael Miller

All rights reserved. No part of this book,
in part or in whole, may be reproduced, transmitted,
or utilized, in any form or by any means, electronic or mechanical,
including photocopying, recording, or by any information storage
and retrieval system, without permission in writing
from the publisher, except for brief quotations
in critical articles, books and reviews.

ISBN 13: 978-0-9989393-3
ISBN 10: 0-9989393-3-1

Pyramid Press First Edition 2024

The paper used in this publication meets the minimum requirements
of the American National Standard for Permanence of
Paper for Printed Library Materials Z39.48-1984

Printed in USA

PYRAMID PRESS
2046 Hillhurst Avenue
Los Angeles, CA 90027
contact@pyramidpress.net

LOVE OF DOGS

DR. MICHAEL MILLER

PYRAMID PRESS
LOS ANGELES, CALIFORNIA, U.S.A.

Dedicated to My Alvin

It's been so long and I still miss him every day. And It's been a very rough stretch lately. After losing Alvin in the prime of his life, age 6, we lost the "originals" Killer age 14, Spanky age 13, and Big Boy age 15. We also lost Princess (Alvin's Mother), rather unexpectedly, along the way. We have quite a collection of ceramic paw prints and urns of ashes in a special place near the front door.

One advantage of having a lot of dogs is you don't have time for a pity party. You have to go on for the others and the youngsters don't understand any other way. They make us stay focused on them, and in the present, and for that I am very grateful.

I also want to remember some people that lost their best friend recently: Jeff Mandon, Kris Wyatt, Rayn Gravelly, Nathaniel Lewis, Roberto Fisher, Christine Minnig, Ryan and Stephanie Teeter.

Table of Contents

The Best of Friends   1

Love   31

Grief   61

In Memory of
Spanky

He gave me 14 years of nothing but love and happiness.

The Best of Friends

*Dogs' lives are far too short.
Really their biggest fault.*

When I look into the eyes of an animal
I do not see an animal.
I see a living being.
I see a friend.
I feel a soul.

Whoever said you
can't buy happiness
doesn't know about
dogs and pig ears.

Life is short–play with your dog.

If your dog doesn't like someone,
you probably shouldn't either.

Compassion for animals is deeply associated with good character, and it may be asserted that he who is cruel to animals cannot be a good man.

Dogs are God's way of apologizing for your relatives.

Dogs make everything better.

The older you get, the more you realize
you have no desire for drama, conflict or stress.
You just want a cozy home, a quiet life
and to be surrounded by lots of dogs
who make you happy.

If the kindest souls were rewarded
with the longest lives then dogs
would outlive us all.

When a ninety pound dog
licks your tears away,
then tries to sit on your lap,
it's hard to feel lonely or sad.

Life is too short to just have one dog.

Dogs make all the bad stuff go away.
Some people don't understand
why my dog means so much to me.
That's okay. My dog does.

An Indian legend says:
"When a human dies, there is a bridge
they must cross to enter into heaven.
At the head of the bridge waits every animal that
human encountered during their lifetime.
The animals, based on what they know of
this person, decide which humans may cross
the bridge...and which are turned away."
That would be Karma at it's finest.

My dogs are the reason I wake up every morning.
And really early, every morning.

They don't care what car you drive...
They don't care who you know...
They don't care what you wear...
They don't care where you live...
They only care that you're there.

The only touch a dog should ever feel is one of kindness.

A dog is one of the few things in life
that is as it seems.

Dogs have a way of finding the people
who need them most.

I'm home forever...
I don't have to be scared anymore.
I am a dog advocate because as a child,
I looked into a dog's eyes,
And saw a soul as real as mine.

Our perfect companions never have fewer than four feet. Such short lives our pets have to spend with us, and they spend most of it waiting for us to come home each day.

The next time you look into your dogs eyes look deep and long. You will see their inner beauty and feel their inner soul.

You think dogs will not be in heaven? I tell you, they will be there long before any of us.
– Pastor Misi

If I had a dollar for every time
my dog made me smile
I would be a millionaire.

Hoberleigh, Age 2 months

Always take care of your dog.
Even if your world falls apart,
he will still be there for you.

I'm telling you, I'm not a dog...
My mom said, I'm a baby...
My mom is always right.

The difference between humans and animals? Animals would never allow the dumbest ones to lead the pack.

There are friendships imprinted in our hearts that will never be diminished by time and distance.

No matter how little money
and how few possessions you own,
having a dog makes you rich.

Happiness is when you look at your dog
and forget all your problems.

No matter how talented, rich
or intelligent you are,
How you treat animals tells me
All I need to know about you.

The greatest fear dogs know is the fear
that you will not come back when you
go out the door without them.

I went to the cinema the other day and in the front row was an old man and with him was his dog. It was a sad funny kind of film, you know the type. In the sad part, the dog cried his eyes out and in the funny part, the dog laughed its head off. This happened all the way through the film. After the film ended, I decided to go and speak to the man. "That's the most amazing thing I've seen," I said. "That dog really seemed to enjoy the film."

The man turned to me and said, "Yeah, it is. He hated the book."

Author Unknown

If it wasn't for dogs, some people would never go for a walk.

Little pup, big world.

Everyone thinks they have the best dog, and none of them are wrong.

If aliens saw us walking our dogs and picking up their poop, who would they think is in charge?

Dogs are not our whole life,
but they make our lives whole.

Love

Love is just a word until someone special comes along and gives it meaning.

The love of my dog is worth every dog hair, every muddy paw print, every plant chewed, every hole dug, every early morning, and every dollar spent.

What a beautiful world it would be if people had hearts like dogs.

A dog is the only thing on earth that loves you more than he loves himself.

No one can fully understand the meaning of love unless he's owned a dog. A dog can show you more honest affection with a flick of his tail than a man can gather through a lifetime of hugs and handshakes.

If I could choose between loving you and breathing... I would use my last breath to say I LOVE YOU.

A best friend is someone who loves you when you forget to love yourself.

My sunshine doesn't come from the skies.
It comes from the love that's in my dogs eyes.

I think dogs are the most amazing creatures;
they give unconditional love.
For me, they are the perfect role model
for being alive.

If you have one friend who would sit
and wait for you without knowing
whether you would come back,
it's your dog. Cherish that love.

Love is a four-legged word.

A dog can teach you more about love than any human being could.

All you need is love and a dog.

They love you so much
they will wait forever for you…
and be thrilled whenever
you show up.

People who love animals are definitely my favorite kind of people.

They love to play ball.

A dog will make you laugh harder and love harder, and give more joy than you ever thought possible.

My biggest accomplishment in life will never be money. It will be all the animals I loved and saved.

Dogs teach us a lot of things, but most of all, they teach us how to love unconditionally.

My dog is not just a dog, he's my best friend.

The more people I meet, the more I love my dog.

Puppies are like rainbows,
they bring color to your life.

"And so, the snuggles and treats begin."

Puppy love is the best thing in and of the world.

Dogs are a reminder
that even in
our darkest moments,
there is always love
and joy to be found.

The best therapist has fur and four legs.

The only thing better than a dog is a puppy.

A puppy keeps you focused entirely
in the precious present.

A lover will give you a kiss...
A friend will give you a hug...
But a dog will give you his heart.

Better than all of the gold in the world,
better than diamonds, better than pearls,
better than any material thing,
is the love of a dog and the joy that it brings.

A dog's love is unconditional, pure, and 100% genuine. They are the epitome of true love and loyalty.

If love could have saved you,
you would have lived forever.

I don't judge others.
I don't hate.
I don't discriminate.
I don't care about money.
I don't hold grudges.
I DO know how to love unconditionally
And that's all I want in return.
I wait for you everyday.
I am your fur-ever friend.

Please don't stop loving me because I get old. I'll always love you!

When I am Old

When I am old...
I will wear soft gray sweatshirts...
and a bandanna over my silver hair...
and I will spend my social security checks on my dogs.

I will sit in my house on my well-worn chair
and listen to my dogs breathing.
I will sneak out in the middle of a
warm summer night and take my dogs
for a run, if my old bones will allow...

When people come to call,
I will smile and nod
as I show them my dogs...
and talk of them and about them...
...the ones so beloved of the past
and the ones so beloved of today...

I will still work hard cleaning after them,
mopping and feeding them and whispering
their names in a soft loving way.
I will wear the gleaming sweat on my throat,
like a jewel, and I will be an embarrassment
to all...especially my family...who have not yet
found the peace in being free
to have dogs as your best friends...

These friends who always wait,
at any hour, for your footfall...
and eagerly jump to their feet
out of a sound sleep,
to greet you as if you are a God,
with warm eyes full of
adoring love and hope
that you will always stay.

I'll hug their big strong necks...
I'll kiss their dear sweet heads...
and whisper in their ears,
you're very special company....

I look in the mirror...
and see I am getting old....
this is the kind of person I am...
and have always been.

Loving dogs is easy. They are the best part of me.

Please accept me for who I am.
My dogs appreciate my presence in their lives...
they love my presence in their lives...

When I am old this will be important to me...
you will understand when you are old,
if you have dogs to love too.

Grief

I am here.
I will always be near you
to calm your broken heart
and to help you smile
at the memories."

You are not there to greet me at the door.
Or lick my tears or make me laugh.
But you are always in my heart, forever.

Goodbyes are not forever.
Goodbyes are not the end.
They simply mean
I'll miss you,
Until we meet again.

All I want is for all my pets in heaven to know how much I love them and miss them.

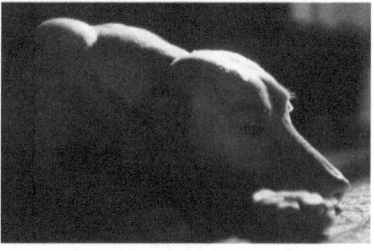

Having a dog will bless you with many of the happiest days of your life, and one of the worst.

Dogs come into our lives to teach us about love and loyalty. They depart to teach us about loss. A new dog never replaces an old dog; it merely expands the heart.

There are moments in life
when you miss your dog so much
you just want to pick them up
from your dreams and
hug them for real.

Believing we will see them again doesn't change
the pain that they're not here now.

You helped me through
the darkest moments of my life:
I don't think I would have
made it without you.

When the time comes to say goodbye to your pet, whisper, "Thank you. I let you go and I celebrate your time with me."

A dog is the only thing that can mend a crack in your broken heart.

My Beloved Pet

I love you and miss you with all my heart
Sending hugs to you reaching over the Rainbow Bridge.
Forever would not have been enough.

If I was granted one wish it would be that my best friend could live forever.

How lucky am I to have something that makes saying goodbye so hard.

The saddest moment is when the one who gave you the best memories becomes a memory.

It is impossible to forget a dog that gave you
so much to remember.

Don't forget,
somewhere between
hello and goodbye,
there was love,
so much love.

Grief never ends…But it changes.
It's a passage, not a place to stay.
Grief is not a sign of weakness,
nor a lack of faith…
It is the price of love.

Those we love do not leave us.
They walk beside us every day.
Unseen and silent but always near,
Still loved, still missed and
Forever dear.

When you feel me
in your heart,
just look up.
I will be right there.

A good dog never dies. He always stays.
He walks beside you on crisp autumn days
when frost is on the fields and winter's
drawing near.

I know that you can't see me,
but trust me I'm right here.
Although I'm up in heaven,
my love for you stays near.

So often I see you crying,
many times you call my name.
I want so much to lick your face
and ease some of your pain.

There will always be that dog that no dog will replace, the dog that will make you cry even when it's been gone for more years than it could ever have lived. It's not the same when one day they're gone.

May the sun set this beautiful night, and may it raise one day upon a world where no animal is laid to rest merely because it has no place to call home. Raise your paws and your voices and pray that one day all shelters will be true safe havens for all of the wonderful animals.

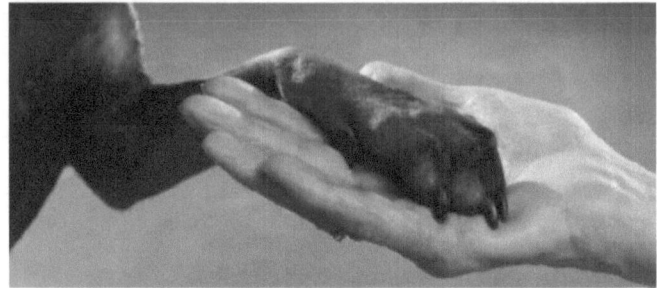

You are no longer where you were.
But you are everywhere I am.

Don't Cry For Me, Mom. I'm Okay!
I can run like a puppy and I can even fly with my new wings!

I wish that I could make you see
that Heaven indeed is real.

That moment when I knew it was time,
but I didn't want it to be.
I wanted to go for a walk again,
or a drive to our favorite park.
There are no words for how sad I am
and your ears are wet with my tears.
I will always remember you
and miss our time together.
I learned to be me with you at my side.

If you could see me run and play
how much better you would feel.
But our loving God has promised me
that when the time is right,
you'll step out of the darkness
and meet me in the light.

Today You Set Me Free

Today you did the bravest thing
Today you set me free
Thank you for showing me
the ultimate dignity.

I'm sorry that my leaving
has broken your kind hearts
But we knew this day would come
The day we had to part.

Don't think I did not hear
every last loving word you said
Don't think I didn't feel
your gentle touch upon my head.

Today you did the bravest thing
Today you set me free.
Thank you for a wonderful life
Thank you for loving me.

All my Love,
Your Dog

I died today.

But yesterday, I lived.

And the day before that,

Week after week,

Year after year, I lived.

I died today.

Not by the hands of harm

But held in the arms of love.

But yesterday, I lived.

Until I was robbed of more tomorrows.

I lived becaused I was loved.

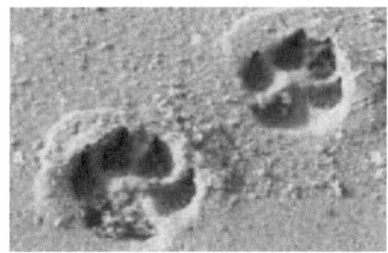

Say Their Name

Every time we say their name,
we affirm their everlasting place in our hearts.
They are not shadows in the mist but bright
lights guiding us, remembered always,
forgotten never.

I Will Wait For You

I came to you late last night,

to be with you while you slept.

I lay my head on your pillow,

while next to me you wept.

A gentle smile kissed your lips,

as I licked away a tear.

Until your time to join me,

I'll be waiting through the years.

Just know I will never judge you

for helping me leave when my body failed.

In my mind you gave me

the ultimate gift of love.

    –Your Dog

I'm not there with you today
but know that I haven't gone astray.
I am the wind blowing through your hair
and the warmth you feel in the air.
When that smile creeps on your face,
remember that I am in a good place.
And when you're feeling sad and down,
recall memories of me running around.
You don't need to look low and high,
just search way deep inside.
And know that we'll never be apart,
for I have left my paw prints on your heart.

Waiting at the Door

I was just a pup when we first met.
I loved you from the start.
You picked me up and took me home
And placed me in your heart.
Good times we had together.
We shared all life could throw,
But the years passed all too quickly,
And my time has come to go.
I know how much you miss me,
I know your heart is sore.
I see the tears that fall when
I'm not waiting at the door.
You always did your best for me;
Your love was plain to see.
And even though it broke your heart
You set my spirit free.
So please be brave without me,
One day we'll meet once more,
For when you're called to Heaven
I'll be waiting at the door.

If I could have just one more cuddle.

Just a Dog

From time to time, someone will tell me: "Hold up, it's just a dog" or "That's a lot of money for just a dog". They don't understand the distance traveled, the time spent, or the costs involved for "just a dog". Some of my happiest moments have come to exist with "just a dog". Many hours have passed and my only company was "just a dog", and I never once feel slighted. In some of my saddest moments I have been kept company by "just a dog" and in those days of darkness, the gentle touch of "just a dog" gave me comfort and reason to overcome the day. If you too think, it's "just a dog", then you will probably understand phrases like "just a friend", "just a sunrise" or "just a promise".

"Just a dog" has taught me the very essence of friendship, trust, and pure unbridled joy.
"Just a dog" brings out the compassion and patience that make me a better person. Because of "just a dog", I will rise early, take long walks and plan for my future. So for me and people like me, it's not "just a dog" but an embodiment of all the hopes and dreams of the future, the fond memories of the past, and often the pure joy of the moment. "Just a dog" brings out what's good in me and diverts my thoughts away from myself and the worries of the day. I hope that someday people can understand that it's not "just a dog", but it's the very thing that gives me humanity and keeps me from being "just a man". So the next time you hear the phrase "just a dog", just smile...
Because they "just don't understand."

They Tell You Not to Cry

They tell you that it's just a dog, not a human being.

They tell you that the pain will be over.

They tell you that the animals don't know that they have to die.

They tell you that it's important not to let him suffer.

They tell you that you can have another one.

They tell you it's going to happen to you.

But they don't know how many times you've looked into your dog's eyes.

They don't know how many times you and your dog have looked into the darkness alone.

They don't know how many times your dog was the only one who was by your side.

They don't know how much fear you have at night when you wake up with your grief.

They don't know how many times your dog slept near you.

They don't know how much you've changed since the dog has become a part of your life.

They don't know how many times you hugged him when he was sick.

They don't know how many times you've acted like you didn't see his hair getting whiter.

They don't know how many times you've talked to your dog; the only one who really hears.

They don't know that it was just your dog who knew you were in pain.

They don't know what it feels like to see your old dog trying to get up to say hello.

They don't know that if things went wrong, the only one who didn't go is your dog.

They don't know that your dog trusts you every moment of his life, even in the last.

They don't know how much your dog loved you and how it is enough for him to be happy because you loved him.

They don't know that crying for a dog is one of the noblest, most significant, true, purest and warmest things you can do.

They don't know when the last time you moved him with trouble...making sure it didn't hurt him.

They don't know what it felt like to pet their face in the last moments of their life...

*In Memory of all those who went
over the rainbow bridge. You all
have a place forever in our hearts.
I loved you your whole life.
I'll miss you for the rest of mine.*

Treasured Friend

I lost a treasured friend today
The little dog who used to lay
Her gentle head upon my knee
And shared her silent thoughts with me.

She'll come no longer to my call
Retrieve no more her favorite ball
A voice far greater than my own
Has called her to his golden throne.

Although my eyes are filled with tears
I thank him for the happy years
He let her spend down here with me
And for her love and loyalty.

When it is time for me to go
And join her there, this much I know
I shall not fear the transient dark
For she will greet me with a bark.

I Love You

I stood by your bed last night,
I came to have a peep.
I could see that you were crying
You found it hard to sleep.
I whined to you softly
as you brushed away a tear,
"It's me, I haven't left you,
I'm well, I'm fine, I'm here."
I was close to you at breakfast,
I watched you pour the tea,
You were thinking of the many times,
your hands reached down to me.
I was with you at the shops today,
Your arms were getting sore.
I longed to take your parcels,
I wish I could do more.
I was with you at my grave today,
You tend it with such care.
I want to re-assure you,
that I'm not lying there.
I walked with you towards the house,
as you fumbled for your key.
I gently put my paw on you,
I smiled and said " it's me."
You looked so very tired,

and sank into a chair.
I tried so hard to let you know,
that I was standing there.
It's possible for me,
to be so near you everyday.
To say to you with certainty,
"I never went away."
You sat there very quietly,
then smiled, I think you knew...
In the stillness of that evening,
I was very close to you.
The day is over...
I smile and watch you yawning
And say "good-night, God bless,
I'll see you in the morning."
And when the time is right for you
to cross the brief divide,
I'll rush across to greet you
and we'll stand, side by side.
I have so many things to show you,
there is so much for you to see.
Be patient, live your journey out...
then come home to be with me...

Letter from Heaven

It's me. I know you're finding it difficult to deal without me, but I'm still around. Remember when my collar fell from the hook yesterday? That was me. I was hoping you would go for a walk outside or something, but you didn't. I miss seeing you smile. You used to have such a bright one, but it hasn't shown lately. Please smile again.

Yesterday I saw that you packed up all my toys and placed them in a box; that's okay. I have plenty of toys up here to play with now. I still kiss your cheeks in the morning, my little nose is probably still cold to your touch. When you sit for your morning coffee, I sit and beg for food at your knee. I know you leave some scrapings down for me still. You got angry when the neighbors dog played with my favorite stick, but that's because he can see me and we were playing in the yard and we didn't mean any harm.

It seems as though the people you work with don't understand the pain you feel.

This makes you think that your sadness isn't valid.
It is. Just because I was a dog, doesn't mean
I didn't have a large impact on your life.

Feel your feelings and don't hold them back
from anyone, especially yourself. Talk about me.
Remember all the silly things I used to do, like
lifting one ear up at the strange sight of my
own reflection in the mirror.

Think of all the car rides and walks we took
together. Remember all the times when you
would have to force me to go outside in the rain
just to go pee. Think of all the different ways
you used to try to sweet talk me when I was
either visiting the vet, or getting groomed;
you know how much I disliked those trips.

Most importantly, I want you to remember
how much I loved you and that I always will.
Thank you for all the treats, head scratches,
cuddles and kisses. It's time that I become your
angel now instead.

~ So much love from the other side of the rainbow,
    Your Best Friend

My Dear Human

My dear human, I see you crying, because it's time for me to leave. Please don't cry. I want to explain some things to you. You're sad that I'm gone, but I'm glad to have met you. How many dogs like me die every day without having met someone special like you! I know you are saddened by my departure, but I had to leave now.

I want to ask you not to blame yourself. I heard you sobbing that you should have done something more for me. Don't say that. You've done a lot for me! Without you, I would have known nothing of the beauty I carry with me today. You must know that dogs live intensely in the present. Our lives begin when we know love, the same love you gave me, my wingless angel.

Please don't cry anymore. I leave happy.
I remember the name you gave me, the warmth
of your house which at that time became mine.
I carry in my heart every caress you gave me.
Wash your face and start smiling.
There are many like me waiting
for someone like you.

A Dog's Last Will and Testament

Before humans die, they write their last will and
testament, give their home and all they have
to those they leave behind. If, with my paws,
I could do the same, this is what I'd ask.

To a poor and lonely stray I'd give my happy home;
my bowl and cozy bed, soft pillow and all my toys;
the lap, which I loved so much; the hand that stroked
my fur; and the sweet voice that spoke my name.

I'd will to the sad, scared shelter dog the place I had
in my human's loving heart, of which there seemed
no bounds.

So, when I die, please do not say, "I will never
have a dog again, for the loss and pain is more
than I can stand."

Instead, go find an unloved dog, one whose life has
held no joy or hope, and give my place to him.

This is the only thing I can give…
The love I left behind.

Alvin is One More Dog in Heaven

I often used to tell you
as you rooted through the bin,
you will never go to Heaven
for to steal is such a sin.
You thought it fun to roll in mud,
to jump in every pool,
but would you come to take a bath?
'As stubborn as a mule!'
I sometimes used to ask you why,
when something else you'd chew,
'of all the dogs in all the world
I'd ended up with you.'
And now the years have slipped away,
your heart it beats no more,
I sit beside your empty bed,
your paw prints on the floor.
And as my heart it breaks in two
one truth with which I'm blessed,
There's one more dog in heaven now,
My friend…You were the best!

In Memory of **My Alvin**
June 24, 2015 - January 7, 2021

No longer by my side but forever in my heart.

How beautiful it is to find someone who asks for nothing but your company.

Alvin and the Originals in the basketball gym.